Quick 'N' Easy
Learning Tasks

by Charlene Howells Lutz

illustrated by Patricia Briles

Fearon Teacher Aids
a division of
David S. Lake Publishers
Belmont, California

Publisher: Mel Cebulash
Editorial director: Ina Tabibian
Editor: Diane K. Whitworth
Managing editor: Susan J. Riddle
Production editor: Stephen Feinstein
Design director: Eleanor Mennick
Designer: Colleen Forbes
Manufacturing director: Casimira Kostecki

ISBN-0-8224-5653-2

Library of Congress Catalog Card Number: 85-50474

Printed in the United States of America

1. 9 8 7 6 5 4 3 2 1

Contents

Introduction

This book provides busy teachers with quality, quick and easy lessons to supplement the classroom curriculum in the areas of language arts, reading, spelling, math, social studies, science, health, handwriting, and art. The tasks are open ended so that teachers may adapt them to best suit their instructional objectives. Because the activities are delightfully illustrated and quick and easy to do, students as well as teachers should enjoy these learning tasks.

While recommended for use with grades one through four, the worksheets can easily be adapted to higher or lower grade levels or adjusted to accommodate students' individual learning requirements. The activities have been tried, tested, and proven successful during my eleven years of public school teaching of both regular and special education students. Since the tasks are interesting and quick and easy to do, they are well suited for students with short attention spans.

With the help of the very talented illustrator Patricia Briles, I have developed 90 learning-task worksheets, 10 for each content area. Each reproducible student worksheet is accented with delightful cartoon characters that students can color after they have completed the task. A teacher's guide, provided at the beginning of each of the nine sections, lists materials and procedures and includes special notes for the teacher. A student award certificate and poster are provided at the end of each section. The teacher can display the poster on the bulletin board or make copies of it and distribute them for the students to color and keep. The award certificate can also be reproduced and distributed as the teacher deems appropriate.

To begin, choose a task, a poster, and an award. Make copies for each of your students and liven up your curriculum the **Quick 'N' Easy** way!

Charlene Howells Lutz

Language Arts Tasks

Motivate your students with the poster, "Language Arts Is the Way." Give the award to students who deserve recognition for their creativity and effort.

Special Reminders and Extra Materials

Task 4 Fortune Exchange: Each student will need scissors and a piece of lined paper.

Task 6 Friendship Card: The worksheet should be duplicated on heavy paper for durability. Provide each student with scissors and crayons or colored markers.

Task 7 Rainy Day, and **Task 8** Trading Places: Each student should have crayons or colored markers.

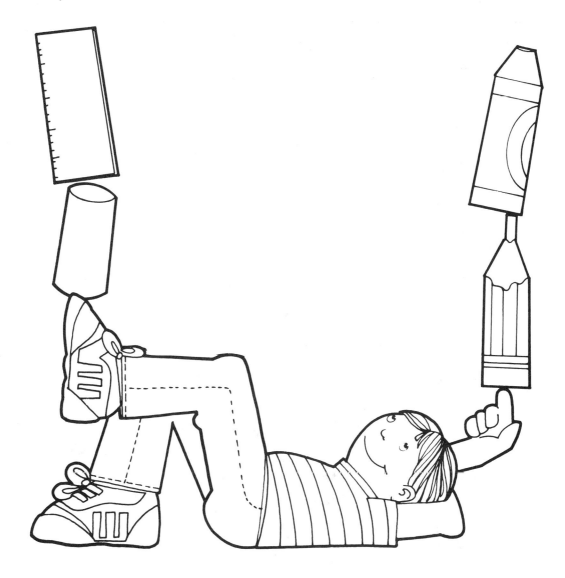

School Days Word Search

Find these school words in the puzzle and circle them. Read across and down.

clock	books	paper	eraser
crayons	bell	desk	teacher
student	ruler	chalk	pencil

```
T E A C H E R R B E L L
Q W E R T Y U I O P A S
A D F G C X B O O K S P
F A D F H D F P A P E R
D E S K A S F G H S O C
P Z X C L V B R N T M R
E R T Y K U E U J U K A
N X C V B N M L W D L Y
C S A F G H J E K E E O
I Z E R A S E R Q N L N
L C L O C K C B N T E S
```

Quick 'N' Easy Learning Tasks, copyright © 1986 David S. Lake Publishers

Homonym Word Search

There are homonyms for these words hidden in the puzzle below. Find the homonyms and circle them. Read across and down.

for	too	herd	right
eight	blew	won	weak
know	bear	meat	see
deer	be		

F O U R O H T W O H
A S Q W N R T S K E
W E E K E W Y E I A
A S D F G R H A K R
L Z X C V I B N M D
N B E E D T M E E T
O Y S U B E P L J K
A S E D A G H A T E
Y B A N R D X C T O
B L U E E C D E A R

Sentence Wheels

Arrange the words in each wheel to form a sentence. Write each sentence correctly below the wheel.

My
is
today
birthday

baked
Mother
cake
a
for
me

said
I
She
could
party
a
have

We
played
food
good
games
and
ate

punctuation

Quick 'N' Easy Learning Tasks, copyright © 1986 David S. Lake Publishers

Fortune Exchange

Write some fortunes. Cut them out and exchange them with your friends. On another piece of paper, write a short story about one of the fortunes you received.

Rhyme Time

Read these two-line poems:

I like bread,
but not in bed.

Don't speak to mice,
'cause they aren't nice.

Now think of two other lines that make a rhyme.
See how many two-line poems you can create.
Write them below.

_____

_____

_____

_____

_____

_____

_____

_____

_____

_____

_____

_____

Quick 'N' Easy Learning Tasks, copyright © 1986 David S. Lake Publishers

Friendship Card

Make a friendship card for someone you like. First cut out your card and fold it in half. Then write words to tell why you like your friend. Draw pictures to go with your words. Sign your name and deliver the card to your friend.

Name _____

Rainy Day

Think about what you like to do on a rainy day. Write a story and draw a picture about that day.

Name _____

Trading Places

What if you could trade places with another student anywhere in the world? Think of some faraway place you would like to be. Write about what your life would be like if you lived there. Draw a picture of that place.

_____

_____

_____

_____

_____

Name _____

Mystery Story

Finish the incomplete sentence below by writing a word in the blank. Then add more sentences to write a short mystery story. Make up a title for your story, too.

    When I got home from school yesterday, I heard strange noises coming from my bedroom. I quietly climbed the stairs and slowly opened the door. Imagine my surprise when I

saw a _____ !

_____

_____

_____

_____

_____

_____

_____

_____

_____

_____

Quick 'N' Easy Learning Tasks, copyright © 1986 David S. Lake Publishers

Name _____

Letter Writer

Write a letter to a friend. Ask some questions so your friend will have a reason to write back to you. Remember to sign your name. Cut out your letter and deliver it.

_____
(date)

Dear _____ ,
(greeting)

_____

_____

_____

_____

_____

_____

_____

_____

_____

_____ ,
(closing)

_____
(signature)

_____

is a fantastic
writer!

_____

is a fantastic
writer!

Language Arts Poster **13**

Reading Tasks

Encourage students to read for enjoyment with the poster, "Read—For the Fun of It!" Give the award to students who deserve recognition for extra reading or special achievement.

Special Reminders and Extra Materials

Task 1 What Do You Think?: The answers are: 1) Yes; 2) Yes; 3) No; 4) Yes; 5) Yes; 6) No; 7) Yes; 8) Yes; 9) Yes; 10) No; 11) No; 12) No; 13) Yes; 14) No; 15) Yes.

Task 4 What Am I?: The answers are: 1) fish; 2) seesaw; 3) saw; 4) bird; 5) umbrella; 6) refrigerator; 7) clown.

Task 5 Following Directions: Each student needs crayons or colored markers.

Task 8 Colorful Words, and **Task 9** More Colorful Words: Provide each student with a dictionary.

The answers for Task 8 are: 1) second; 2) yes; 3) no; 4) judo, karate, or a related sport; 5) yes; 6) no; 7) ice hockey; 8) no; 9) oil; 10) no.

The answers for Task 9 are: 1) no; 2) buy something; 3) drink; 4) be wounded in the service; 5) no; 6) jealousy; 7) in a theater; 8) no; 9) gardening; 10) Answers will vary.

Name _____

What Do You Think?

Answer the questions. Write Yes or No in the blanks.

1. Can you eat a cookie? _____

2. Can you smell with your nose? _____

3. Do you have three ears? _____

4. Is the sun hot? _____

5. Do you chew with your teeth? _____

6. Does a cow have two tails? _____

7. Can you fly in an airplane? _____

8. Can you see a tiger at the zoo? _____

9. Can you read a book? _____

10. Do you have purple hair? _____

11. Do you wear a belt on your head? _____

12. Does a bear have wings? _____

13. Is an apple a fruit? _____

14. Does a duck have fur? _____

15. Can you sit in a chair? _____

Name _____

Reading to Find Out

Read the story. Answer the questions. Write your answers in the blanks provided.

Joe got a baseball for his birthday.
He and Larry played catch with it in
   the yard.
Once Larry did not catch the ball.
It rolled into the street.
Joe looked carefully up and down
   the street.
He saw that no cars were coming.
He quickly picked up the ball and ran
   back to the yard.

1. Who got something for his birthday? _____

2. What did he get? _____

3. Who did Joe play catch with? _____

4. Who did not catch the ball? _____

5. Where did the ball roll? _____

6. Who picked up the ball from the street? _____

7. What did he do before running into the street? _____

_____

Quick 'N' Easy Learning Tasks, copyright © 1986 David S. Lake Publishers

Picture Clues

Read the incomplete sentences below. Fill in the blanks with words shown by the picture clues.

1. You can tie your _____ .

2. You can sleep in a _____ .

3. You can fly a _____ .

4. You can open a _____ .

5. You can drink _____ .

6. You can drive a _____ .

7. You can read a _____ .

8. You can eat an _____ .

What Am I?

Read the sentences. Draw a line from the sentence to the correct picture.

1. I swim in the water.

2. I go up and down.

3. I cut wood.

4. I have wings.

5. I keep the rain off you.

6. I keep food cold.

7. I can make you laugh.

Following Directions

Follow the directions below. Use crayons or colored markers to complete the pictures.

1. Draw a black hat on Mr. Glen's head.
2. Draw three red buttons on his coat.
3. Color Mr. Glen's pants brown.
4. Color his coat blue.
5. Leave his shoes white.
6. Draw a brown stick in Mr. Glen's hand.

Quick 'N' Easy Learning Tasks, copyright © 1986 David S. Lake Publishers

1. Draw a tail on the cat.
2. Color the cat black.
3. Color its eyes yellow.
4. Draw a bowl of milk to the left of the cat.
5. Draw a mouse to the right of the cat.
6. Color the mouse brown.
7. Draw a wide smile on the cat's face.

Choosing the Right Order I

Read each story below. Then read the sentences that follow each story. Number the sentences in the same order as they happened in the story.

The first day of school was exciting for Tom. First he met his new teacher. Then he played ball with six new friends. Finally, he received a Good Citizen award from his teacher. When Tom arrived home, he told his mother the good news.

_____ Tom received a Good Citizen award.

_____ Tom arrived home.

_____ Tom played ball.

_____ Tom met his new teacher.

Sherry received something special for her birthday. Five friends came to her house for a party. One girl brought her a big box with three small holes in the top. Sherry opened many presents, but saved the big box for last. How surprised she was to find a baby kitten inside!

_____ Sherry opened the big box.

_____ Five friends came to Sherry's house.

_____ Sherry opened many presents.

_____ Sherry found a kitten in the big box.

Choosing the Right Order II

Read each story below. Then read the sentences that follow each story. Number the sentences in the same order as they happened in the story.

Winning the foot race was Sam's greatest thrill! He had practiced long and hard for eight weeks. On the morning of the race Sam ate a light breakfast and rested at home. In the afternoon he and his parents drove to the running track. When Sam's name was called, he lined up at the starting line with the other racers. Sam sprang forward as the starter's gun went off. He dashed down the track. Sam crossed the finish line a winner!

_____ Sam and his parents drove to the running track.

_____ Sam ate breakfast and rested.

_____ Sam won the race.

_____ Sam practiced for eight weeks.

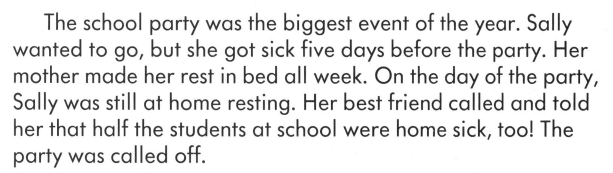

The school party was the biggest event of the year. Sally wanted to go, but she got sick five days before the party. Her mother made her rest in bed all week. On the day of the party, Sally was still at home resting. Her best friend called and told her that half the students at school were home sick, too! The party was called off.

_____ Sally got sick.

_____ Sally's best friend called her.

_____ Sally rested in bed.

_____ The party was called off.

Name _____

Colorful Words

Read the questions below. Look up the underlined words in the dictionary. Then write your answers in the blanks.

1. If you won a <u>red</u> <u>ribbon</u> in a race, did you come in first, second, or third? _____

2. Can you eat <u>red</u> <u>snapper</u>?

   _____

3. Would you want your name on a <u>blacklist</u>? _____

4. If you earn a <u>black</u> <u>belt</u>, what is your sport? _____

5. Could you put a leash on a <u>redbone</u>? _____

6. Is a <u>black-eyed</u> <u>Susan</u> a girl who got in a fight? _____

7. In what sport would you find a <u>blue</u> <u>line</u>? _____

8. Would you chew <u>blue</u> <u>gum</u>? _____

9. What is another name for <u>black</u> <u>gold</u>? _____

10. If you visit your friend once in a <u>blue</u> <u>moon</u>, do you see your friend often? _____

Quick 'N' Easy Learning Tasks, copyright © 1986 David S. Lake Publishers

Name _____

More Colorful Words

Read the questions below. Look up the underlined words in the dictionary. Then write your answers in the blanks.

1. Would you find a <u>yellowhammer</u> in a toolbox? _____

2. What could you do with a <u>greenback</u>? _____

3. Would you drink, play with, or attack <u>orange pekoe</u>? _____

4. What do you do to get a <u>Purple Heart</u>? _____

_____

5. Would you hang a <u>yellow jacket</u> in the closet? _____

6. What is the <u>green-eyed monster</u>? _____

7. Where can you find a <u>greenroom</u>? _____

8. If you are a <u>greenhorn</u> at swimming, would you jump into the deep end of the pool?

_____

9. What are you good at if you have a <u>green thumb</u>? _____

_____

10. Give one example of a <u>redbird</u>.

_____

Name _____

Book Report Pyramid

Read a book of your choice. Then follow these directions to fill in the blanks in the pyramid below.

1. Rename the book in one word.
2. Name two places mentioned in the book.
3. Name three important characters.
4. Describe the book in four words.
5. Write five reasons why others should read this book.
6. Write six new words you learned in this book.

READ · FOR THE FUN OF IT!

Spelling Tasks

Motivate your students to spell correctly with the poster, "Spelling Can Spellbind Your Friends!" Give the award to students who deserve recognition for improvement or achievement on weekly spelling tests.

Special Reminders and Extra Materials

Task 1 Word Cards: The worksheet should be duplicated on heavy paper for durability. Scissors and a list of spelling words are required for each student.

Task 2 Scrambled Words: Provide each student with scissors.

Task 4 Rhyming Words: The answers are: 1) dog; 2) candy; 3) rose; 4) ball; 5) yellow; 6) four; 7) saw; 8) pea.

Task 6 Build-a-Word: Answers will vary since there are more than 15 valid combinations.

Task 9 Spelling Riddles: The answers are: 1) mat; 2) pen; 3) one; 4) door.

Task 10 Spelling Train: Provide each student with a dictionary.

Name _____

Word Cards

Make word cards for your spelling words. Write one word on each card. Then cut out the cards along the dotted lines. Practice spelling your words with a friend.

Quick 'N' Easy Learning Tasks, copyright © 1986 David S. Lake Publishers

Scrambled Words

The color words below have their letters scrambled. Write the words correctly. Use the words in the box if you need help.

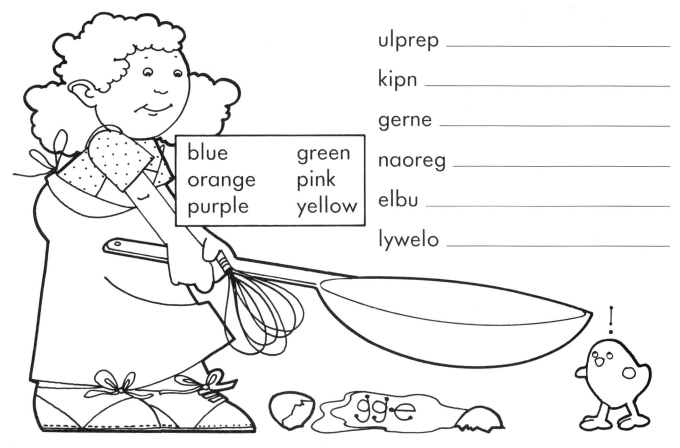

blue	green
orange	pink
purple	yellow

ulprep _____

kipn _____

gerne _____

naoreg _____

elbu _____

lywelo _____

Write five of your spelling words below. Then scramble the letters and write them in the next column. Cut out your scrambled word list and exchange it with a friend.

My five spelling words are:	Scrambled they look like this:
_____	_____
_____	_____
_____	_____
_____	_____
_____	_____

Anagrams

c-h-u-m?

Word pairs like *tan* and *ant* are anagrams. They have exactly the same letters, but in a different order. Write new words by changing the order of the letters in each word below.

eat _____

spot _____

team _____

who _____

mane _____

pan _____

m-u-c-h!

Write some anagram pairs of your own below.

_____   _____

_____   _____

_____   _____

Rhyming Words

Complete the sentences below by writing words that rhyme with the underlined words.

1. A pet that rhymes with <u>log</u> is _____ .

2. A treat that rhymes with <u>dandy</u> is _____ .

3. A flower that rhymes with <u>nose</u> is _____ .

4. A toy that rhymes with <u>hall</u>

   is _____ .

5. A color that rhymes with <u>fellow</u>

   is _____ .

6. A number that rhymes with <u>door</u>

   is _____ .

7. A tool that rhymes with <u>paw</u>

   is _____ .

8. A vegetable that rhymes with <u>sea</u>

   is _____ .

Beginning Sound Clues

Write words that start with the same beginning sounds.

b

d

f

_____

_____

_____

_____

_____

_____

_____

_____

_____

g

m

p

_____

_____

_____

_____

_____

_____

_____

_____

_____

s

t

_____

_____

_____

_____

_____

_____

r

_____

_____

_____

Build-a-Word

Pick a word in Box One and combine it with a word in Box Two to make a new word. Write your new words in the blanks below. All the words you make are names of things found around the house.

BOX ONE		
door	hall	step
bath	stair	tooth
dish	news	cup
cook	bed	tea
fire	book	mail

BOX TWO		
brush	box	shelf
paper	board	room
book	case	way
washer	bell	tub
spoon	place	ladder

1. _____

2. _____

3. _____

4. _____

5. _____

6. _____

7. _____

8. _____

9. _____

10. _____

11. _____

12. _____

13. _____

14. _____

15. _____

Letter Links

Fill in the missing vowels to
make words. All the words
name people or things found
at school.

1. d __ sk

2. b __ ll

3. b __ __ k

4. b __ y

5. cl __ ssr __ __ m

6. g __ rl

7. p __ p __ r

8. p __ nc __ l

9. r __ l __ r

10. sl __ d

Quick 'N' Easy Learning Tasks, copyright © 1986 David S. Lake Publishers

What's Missing?

Write the missing letter on each line.

ca___	ba___	cu___
we___	pi___	bu___
___id	___ar	___um
___ey	___og	___ox

Name _____

Spelling Riddles

Solve the riddles. Write the answers on the lines provided.

1. I rhyme with *hat*.
You wipe your feet on me when
you come inside on a rainy day.

I am a _____.

2. I begin with
the same sound as *pet*.
You can write with me.
I have three letters.

I am a _____.

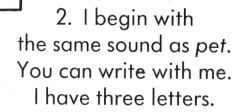

3. If you add me to three,
you get four.

I am _____.

4. I might have a lock.
If I'm closed, you knock.

I am a _____.

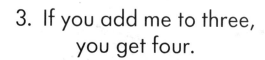

Write a spelling riddle of your
own on the lines below. Give it
to a friend to solve.

_____

_____

_____

_____

Quick 'N' Easy Learning Tasks, copyright © 1986 David S. Lake Publishers

Name _____

Spelling Train

Build onto the spelling train by writing a word that begins with the last letter of the word before it. See how long you can make your train.

team + man + near + _____ + _____ +

_____ + _____ + _____ +

_____ + _____ + _____ +

_____ + _____ + _____ +

_____ + _____ + _____ +

_____ + _____ + _____ +

_____ + _____ + _____ +

_____ + _____ + _____ +

_____ + _____ + _____ +

_____ + _____ + _____

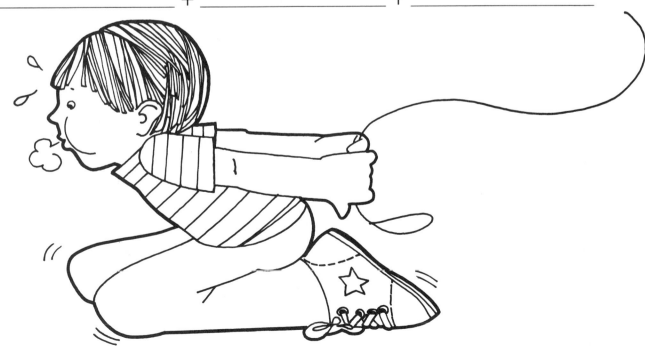

_____

scored
___ on a spelling test
today!

_____

scored
___ on a spelling test
today!

38 Spelling Award

Math Tasks

Arouse student interest in math with the poster, "Math Adds Up!" Give the award to students who deserve recognition for successfully completing these math tasks.

Special Reminders and Extra Materials

Task 1 Follow the Dots, and **Task 3** Color-by-Code: Each student should have crayons or colored markers.

Task 4 Secret Code: The hidden message reads, "In the dictionary."

Task 6 Metric Measure: Provide centimeter rulers and several meter sticks for students to share.

Task 7 Shape Hunt: Students need crayons or colored markers.

Task 8 The Price Is Right: The answers are: 1) 95¢; 2) 50¢; 3) 35¢; 4) $1.50; 5) $1.80; 6) 9; 7) eraser; 8) pencil; 9) ruler, note pad; 10) eraser, pen, pencil.

Task 9 Favorite Pets Bar Graph: The answers are: 1) dogs, fish, hamsters; 2) 10; 3) 4; 4) dogs; 5) 16; 6) hamsters; 7) hamsters; 8) cats.

Task 10 Favorite Fruits Circle Graph: The answers are: 1) apples; 2) 5; 3) 5; 4) oranges; 5) peaches; 6) apples; 7) 40.

Follow the Dots

To find the hidden picture, start at the arrow and draw lines to connect the numbered dots in order. Color your picture.

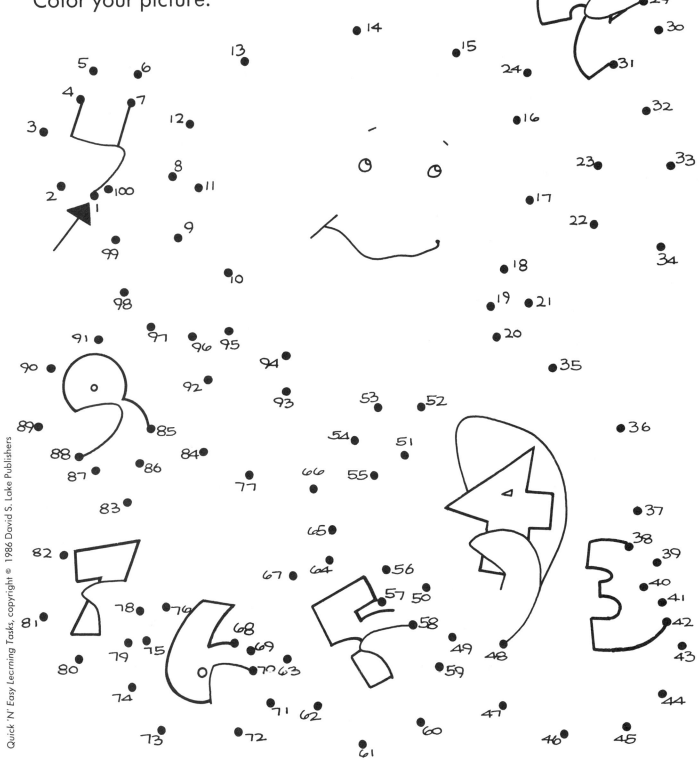

Name _____

Multiplication Maze

Write answers to the multiplication problems. Then find your way through the maze from start to finish. Draw a line to mark your path.

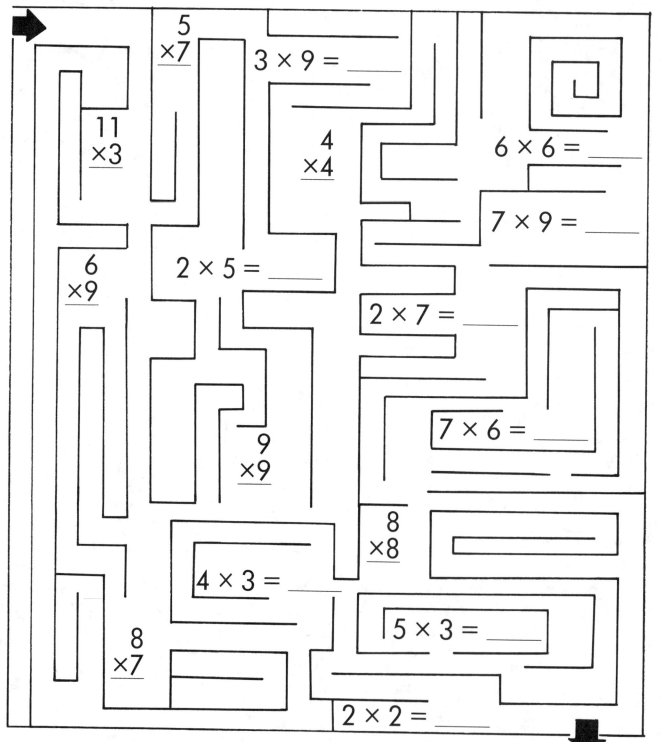

5×7

$3 \times 9 =$ _____

11×3

4×4

$6 \times 6 =$ _____

$7 \times 9 =$ _____

6×9

$2 \times 5 =$ _____

$2 \times 7 =$ _____

9×9

$7 \times 6 =$ _____

8×8

$4 \times 3 =$ _____

$5 \times 3 =$ _____

8×7

$2 \times 2 =$ _____

Color-by-Code

Solve the number problems below.
Then use the code to color
the picture correctly.

ANSWER CODE

1 = red   4 = green
2 = orange   5 = blue
3 = yellow   6 = purple

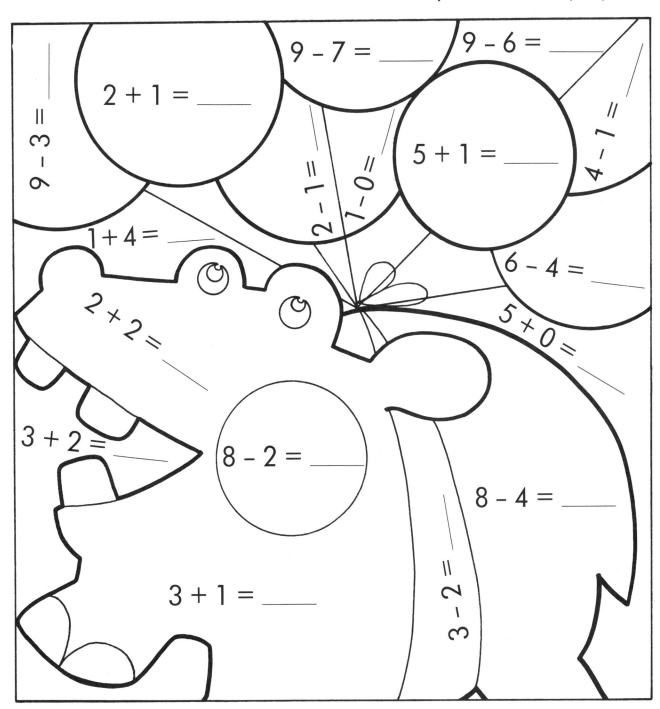

9 – 7 = ____

9 – 6 = ____

2 + 1 = ____

9 – 3 = ____

4 – 1 = ____

2 – 1 = ____

1 – 0 = ____

5 + 1 = ____

1 + 4 = ____

6 – 4 = ____

2 + 2 = ____

5 + 0 = ____

3 + 2 = ____

8 – 2 = ____

8 – 4 = ____

3 – 2 = ____

3 + 1 = ____

Secret Code

Write answers to the problems in the boxes below. To solve the riddle, change your answers into letters by using the answer code. Write the letters on the blanks below the boxes.

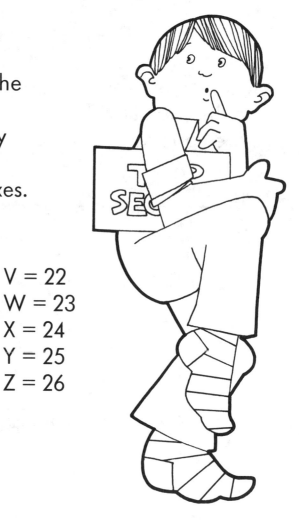

ANSWER CODE

A = 1	H = 8	O = 15	V = 22
B = 2	I = 9	P = 16	W = 23
C = 3	J = 10	Q = 17	X = 24
D = 4	K = 11	R = 18	Y = 25
E = 5	L = 12	S = 19	Z = 26
F = 6	M = 13	T = 20	
G = 7	N = 14	U = 21	

Riddle: Where does Monday come before Sunday?

$$3 \times 3 \qquad 21 - 7 \qquad 5 \times 4 \qquad 4 \times 2 \qquad 10 - 5$$

☐ ☐   ☐ ☐ ☐

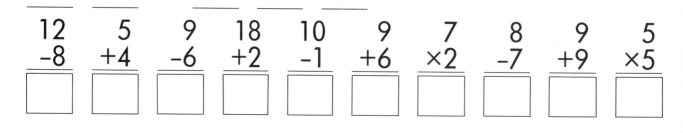

$$12 - 8 \quad 5 + 4 \quad 9 - 6 \quad 18 + 2 \quad 10 - 1 \quad 9 + 6 \quad 7 \times 2 \quad 8 - 7 \quad 9 + 9 \quad 5 \times 5$$

☐ ☐ ☐ ☐ ☐ ☐ ☐ ☐ ☐ ☐

___ ___ ___ ___ ___ ___ ___ ___ ___ ___

Timekeeper

Draw minute and hour hands on each clock to show the correct time.

9:00   3:05   4:45

7:20   11:15   12:30

Write the time you get up, the time you eat lunch, and the time you go to bed. Draw hands on the clocks to show these times.

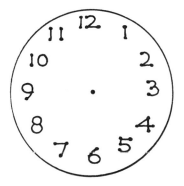   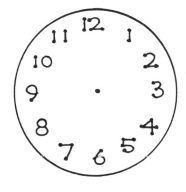   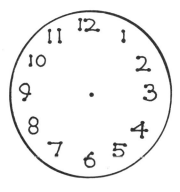

_____   _____   _____

Metric Measure

Measure the following objects to the nearest centimeter or meter. Write your measurements in the blanks below.

1. The length of a pencil is _____ centimeters.

2. The width of a desk top is _____ centimeters.

3. The length of a classroom wall is _____ meters.

4. The length of a little finger is _____ centimeters.

5. The width of a teacher's desk is _____ meters.

6. The height of a classroom door is _____ meters.

7. The length of a shoe is _____ centimeters.

8. The length of a chalkboard is _____ meters.

Quick 'N' Easy Learning Tasks, copyright © 1986 David S. Lake Publishers

Shape Hunt

Find these shapes in the picture:
◯ ☐ △ ▭

Color the ones you find using the code in the box.

SHAPE COLOR CODE

circle ◯ red

square ☐ blue

triangle △ yellow

rectangle ▭ green

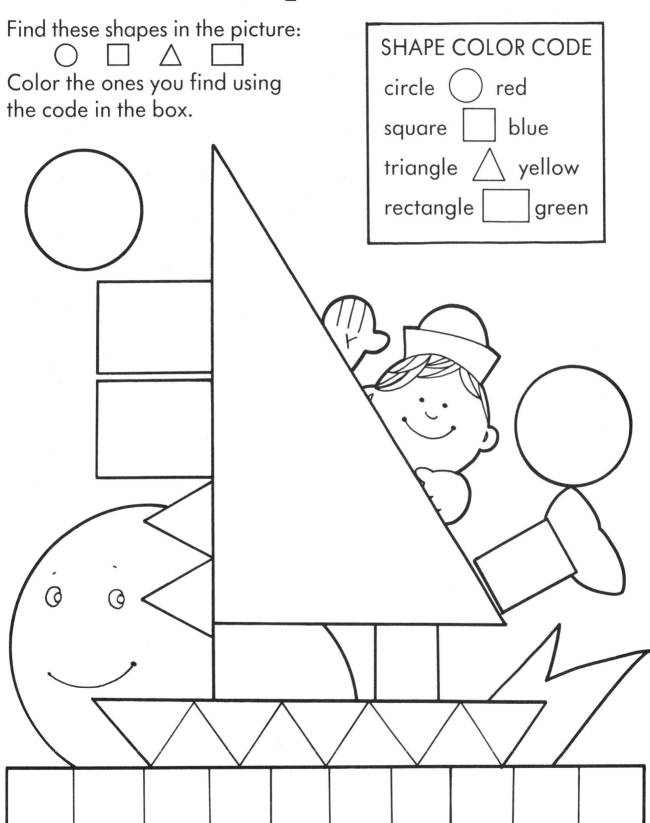

Name _____

The Price Is Right

Use the price list to help answer the problems below.

1. How much would a ruler and a box of crayons cost together?

   _____

2. How much would two pens cost?

   _____

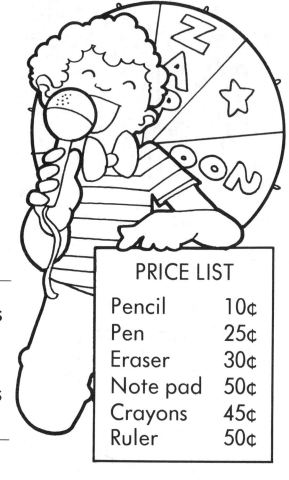

PRICE LIST	
Pencil	10¢
Pen	25¢
Eraser	30¢
Note pad	50¢
Crayons	45¢
Ruler	50¢

3. How much would a pen and a pencil cost together? _____

4. How much would three note pads cost? _____

5. How much would three note pads and one eraser cost? _____
   (Hint: Use answer to #4.)

6. How many pencils could you buy for 90¢? _____

7. If you gave the clerk a dime and a quarter and received a nickel change, what did you buy? _____

8. If you gave the clerk a quarter and received 15¢ change, what did you buy? _____

9. What two items could you buy for exactly $1.00? _____

10. List three different items you could buy for exactly 65¢. _____

   _____

Quick 'N' Easy Learning Tasks, copyright © 1986 David S. Lake Publishers

Favorite Pets Bar Graph

The bar graph shows how many students own each kind of pet. Look at the graph. Then complete the sentences below.

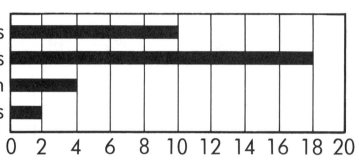

1. The graph shows the number of cats, _____ ,

   _____ , and _____ owned by

   the students.

2. _____ students own cats.

3. _____ students own fish.

4. Which pets are owned by the greatest number of students?

   _____

5. How many more students own dogs than hamsters?

   _____

6. More students own fish than _____ .

7. Which pets are owned by the smallest number of students?

   _____

8. Which pet is owned by 10 students? _____

Quick 'N' Easy Learning Tasks, copyright © 1986 David S. Lake Publishers

Name _____

Favorite Fruits Circle Graph

The circle graph shows how many students like each kind of fruit. Look at the graph. Then complete the sentences below.

1. The most popular fruit is _____ .

2. Only _____ children like peaches.

3. There are _____ more children who like apples than there are who like oranges.

4. The same number of children who like bananas like

    _____ .

5. Fewer children like _____ than like bananas.

6. More children like _____ than like oranges.

7. There are _____ children who voted for their favorite fruits.

Quick 'N' Easy Learning Tasks, copyright © 1986 David S. Lake Publishers

is a
math whiz !

is a
math whiz !

MATH ADDS UP!

Quick 'N' Easy Learning Tasks, copyright © 1986 David S. Lake Publishers

Social Studies Tasks

Stimulate student interest in practicing these social studies skills with the poster, "Social Studies Is Number One!" Give the award to students who deserve recognition for work well done.

Special Reminders and Extra Materials

Task 1 Map Directions: The answers are: 1) north; 2) south; 3) east; 4) south; 5) north; 6) east; 7) west.

Task 2 Map Symbols: The answers are: 1) five; 2) ocean; 3) south; 4) six; 5) yes; 6) mountains.

Task 3 Map Sectors: The answers are: 1) seven; 2) Middleburg, C-1; 3) city, A-3; 4) Blossom; 5) mountain, B-2; 6) B-3; 7) lakes, A-2 and B-2.

Task 6 Community Capers: The answers are: 1) bank; 2) drugstore; 3) furniture store; 4) toy store; 5) library; 6) beauty shop; 7) supermarket; 8) post office; 9) service station; 10) dentist's office; 11) hospital.

Task 7 What's My Line?: The answers are: 1) police officer; 2) barber; 3) mail carrier; 4) nurse; 5) plumber; 6) engineer; 7) carpenter; 8) farmer.

Task 8 Who's Who?: Cut out pictures of community workers from newspapers or magazines. Some possibilities are police, fire fighters, doctors, nurses, teachers, political figures, dentists, gardeners, construction workers, and mail carriers. Put these pictures in a box and have each student choose one to paste on his or her worksheet.

Task 9 Family and Friends: Provide crayons or colored markers for your students.

Task 10 Secret Pals: Make a "Secret Pal" box from a large shoe box. Tape down the lid and cut out a hole large enough for a student's hand to go through. Print each student's name on a piece of paper and put the names in the box. Each student will pick a name from the box and write a letter to his or her secret pal, using the letter form provided. Each student will need scissors.

Name _____

Map Directions

Look at the map. Then fill in each blank below using the word *north*, *south*, *east*, or *west*.

1. The library is _____ of the fire station.

2. The school is _____ of the church.

3. The supermarket is _____ of the library.

4. The drugstore is _____ of the supermarket.

5. The post office is _____ of the church.

6. The bank is _____ of the post office.

7. The school is _____ of the drugstore.

Quick 'N' Easy Learning Tasks, copyright © 1986 David S. Lake Publishers

Map Symbols

Look at the map and fill in the blanks below.

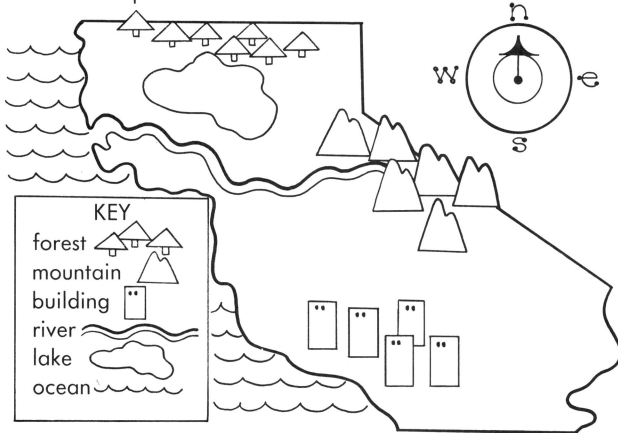

1. How many buildings are there? _____

2. The river flows from the mountains to the

   _____ .

3. Is the lake north, south, east, or west of the forest?

   _____

4. How many mountains are there? _____

5. Is the ocean west of the mountains? _____

6. Are the buildings closer to the lake or the mountains?

   _____

Name _____

Map Sectors

Look at the map and fill in the blanks below.

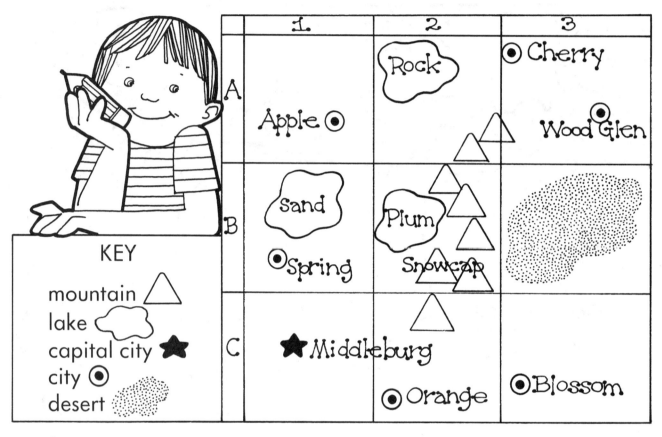

1. There are _____ cities on the map.

2. The capital city is _____ . It is in sector

   _____ .

3. Cherry is a _____ . It is in sector _____ .

4. _____ is in sector C-3.

5. Snowcap is a _____ . It is in sector _____ .

6. The desert is in sector _____ .

7. Rock and Plum are _____ . They are found in

   sectors _____ and _____ .

Quick 'N' Easy Learning Tasks, copyright © 1986 David S. Lake Publishers

Land and Water Forms

Use words in the box to label
the land and water forms on
the map below.

mountains	river	lake
continent	bay	ocean
peninsula	island	gulf

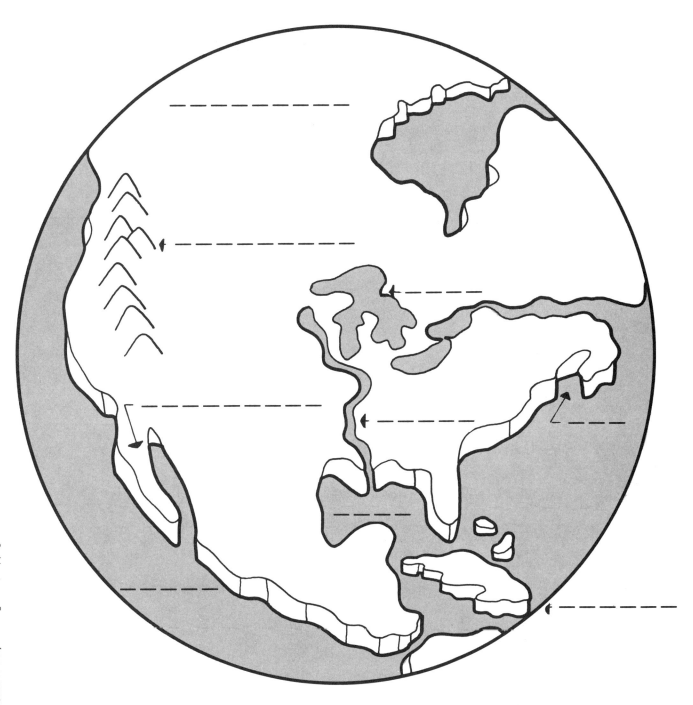

Mapmaker

Draw a map of your classroom. Include big things like students' desks, teacher's desk, tables, extra chairs, closets, cupboards, shelves; and small things like the wastebasket, pencil sharpener, and flag. Use a map key to simplify your drawing.

KEY

Quick 'N' Easy Learning Tasks, copyright © 1986 David S. Lake Publishers

Community Capers

Use the words in the box to fill in the blanks below.

I can

1. cash a check at the _____.
2. buy medicine at the _____.
3. buy a chair at the _____.
4. buy toys at the _____.
5. borrow books from the _____.
6. get a haircut at the _____.
7. buy food at the _____.
8. mail a letter at the _____.
9. buy gas for the car at the _____.
10. get my teeth cleaned at the _____.
11. get help if I hurt myself at the _____.

post office	library	hospital
furniture store	bank	toy store
dentist's office	drugstore	service station
supermarket	beauty shop	

Quick 'N' Easy Learning Tasks, copyright © 1986 David S. Lake Publishers

Name _____

What's My Line?

Read each sentence. Then draw a line to match the sentence with the picture of the person who might have said it.

1. I protect people.

2. I cut your hair.

3. I bring letters.

4. I help sick people.

5. I fix water pipes.

6. I drive the train.

7. I build houses.

8. I grow food.

Name _____

Who's Who?

Find a picture of a community helper.
Paste it in the box below.

This is a picture of a _____.

Write three things you know about this community helper. Use
complete sentences.

1. _____

2. _____

3. _____

Family and Friends

Draw a picture of something you enjoy doing alone.

Draw a picture of something you have fun doing with friends.

Draw a picture of something you like doing with your family.

Name _____

Secret Pals

Pick a name from the "Secret Pal" box. Write a note to your secret pal by filling in the blanks below. Do not sign your name. Cut out your note along the dotted line. Give it to the teacher to deliver for you.

- -

_____
(date)

Dear _____ ,

    I am your secret pal. I can't tell you my name, but I can help you guess who I am. Here are some hints.

    I am _____ years old. My birthday is _____ .

There are _____ members in my family. My favorite color

is _____ . My favorite sport is _____ .

After school I like to _____ .

My best school subject is _____ . I like to eat

_____ . My favorite song is _____

_____ .

_____ makes me happy. _____ makes me sad.

    Do you know who I am? If so, write back to me.

                       Your Secret Pal

_____ is
#1
in social studies!

_____ is
#1
in social studies!

SOCIAL STUDIES

IS NUMBER ONE!

Science Tasks

Arouse students' curiosity with the poster, "Science Is the Real Thing!" Give the award to students who deserve recognition for their scientific accomplishments.

Special Reminders and Extra Materials

Task 1 Scavenger Hunt: Give each student a paper bag. Students will search for items that match the descriptions on the worksheet and collect the items in the paper bags.

Task 2 Science Detective: Give each student a magnifying glass and some objects for viewing. The items collected for Task 1 may be excellent for this task.

Task 3 Weight Watcher: Set up several balance scales for students to use. Also provide six objects which students will list from lightest to heaviest by estimating their weights. They will then weigh the objects and list them by their actual weights.

Task 4 Fingerprint Findings: Reproduce the worksheet on heavy paper for durability. Several ink pads and magnifying glasses are required and can be shared by the students if necessary. Students should wash their hands thoroughly after completing this task.

Task 5 Magnet Mania: Provide each student with a magnet and small objects (some of which must contain iron) for sampling with the magnet.

Task 6 Weather Report: An outdoor thermometer which displays both Fahrenheit and Celsius markings is needed.

Task 7 Popcorn Fun: Buy several bags of popcorn kernels. Give each student two handfuls of kernels to use in checking guesses.

Task 8 Mystery Sounds: You need a tape player, earphones (if students complete this task individually), and a cassette tape on which you will record everyday sounds such as running water, a lawn mower, a baby crying, a washing machine, a vacuum cleaner, car keys rattling, a dog barking, a car motor, and a typewriter.

Task 9 Midas Touch: Make a "mystery box" from a large shoe box. Tape down the lid and cut out a hole large enough for a student's hand to go through. Fill the box with at least ten items that the students will attempt to identify by touch alone. These items might include a spool of thread, a hairbrush, a comb, an eraser, a rock, a pencil, a nail file, a paper clip, a feather, a ruler, and a twig. Students will also classify the objects they identify as manufactured or natural. Remind students not to peek in the box!

Task 10 Forest Ranger: Each student is to bring to class a leaf to study. Provide tree books with close-up pictures of trees and their leaves. Students will use these books to help identify their leaf samples. Each student also needs a piece of paper and a crayon for the leaf rubbing.

Scavenger Hunt

Find ten objects that match the descriptions below. Put them in your paper bag. Then list the ten objects you found. Use the lines provided.

I found something

1. round _____

2. smooth _____

3. soft _____

4. green _____

5. living _____

6. non-living _____

7. shiny _____

8. long _____

9. that doesn't belong outside _____

_____

10. I can't identify _____

_____

Name _____

Science Detective

Your teacher will give you several objects. Look at them closely under the magnifying glass. Draw and label what you see. Show your drawings to a friend, but first cover the labels. Can your friend tell what you observed by your drawings?

1
I looked at _____ .
This is what I saw:

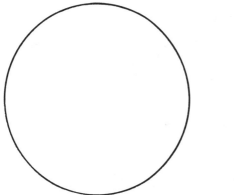

2
I looked at _____ .
This is what I saw:

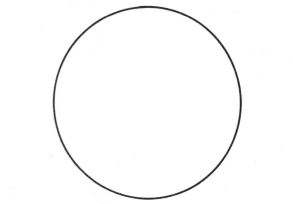

3
I looked at _____ .
This is what I saw:

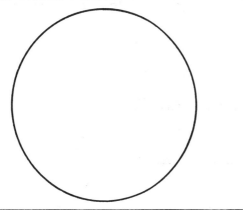

4
I looked at _____ .
This is what I saw:

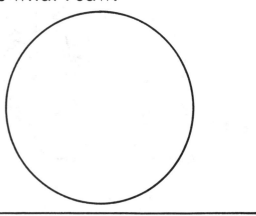

Name _____

Weight Watcher

Choose six objects to weigh. First estimate their weights from lightest to heaviest. List them in that order in column one. Then weigh all the objects on the scale and write their actual weights in column two. Now list the objects correctly from lightest to heaviest in column three. Does column one match column three? If so, you are a great weight watcher!

Order by Estimated Weight	Actual Weight	Order by Actual Weight

Fingerprint Findings

Every person's fingerprints are different. Press your fingertips on an ink pad. Then make a fingerprint of each finger in the proper space below. Examine your prints with a magnifying glass. Notice the patterns. Compare your fingerprints with a friend's. Are any of them similar? How are they different?

LEFT HAND		RIGHT HAND	
Thumb	Forefinger	Thumb	Forefinger
Middle Finger	Ring Finger	Middle Finger	Ring Finger
Little Finger		Little Finger	

↑This is the finger I like best. It is   ↑This is the finger I like best. It is

my _____ finger.   my _____ finger.

Magnet Mania

Get a magnet from your teacher. See how many objects your magnet will attract. List these objects below. Tell what you think all these objects contain.

A magnet attracts these objects:

_____

_____

_____

_____

_____

_____

_____

I think all these objects

contain _____ .

Name _____

Weather Report

Keep a record of the week's weather on the chart below. Fill in the dates. Each day choose a word from the weather box that best describes that day's weather and write it on the chart. Then look at the outside thermometer and write down the temperature in degrees Fahrenheit and Celsius.

WEATHER BOX		
windy	sunny	smoggy
rainy	foggy	
snowy	cloudy	

Day of Week	Monday	Tuesday	Wednesday	Thursday	Friday
Date					
Today's weather is:					
The temperature is:	_____ °F _____ °C	_____ °F _____ °C	_____ °F _____ °C	_____ °F _____ °C	_____ °F _____ °C

Name _____

Popcorn Fun

Guess how many popcorn kernels will fill each shape below. Write your guesses on the lines provided. Then fill in the shapes with the popcorn kernels. Count the number of kernels needed to fill each shape. Now write the actual numbers on the lines provided. See how close your guesses are.

Guess _____

Actual _____

Guess _____

Actual _____

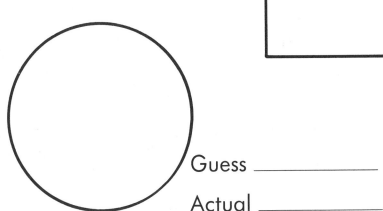

Guess _____

Actual _____

Guess _____

Actual _____

Mystery Sounds

You are going to listen to a tape of different sounds. They all should be familiar to you. As you listen to each mystery sound, try to guess what it is. Write your answers in the blanks below.

Sound 1 _____

Sound 2 _____

Sound 3 _____

Sound 4 _____

Sound 5 _____

Sound 6 _____

Sound 7 _____

Here are some words that describe familiar sounds. Think of something that could cause each sound and write it in the blank provided. Example: bang—a firecracker

1. tick _____

4. hiss _____

2. crash _____

5. rattle _____

3. pop _____

6. boom _____

Quick 'N' Easy Learning Tasks, copyright © 1986 David S. Lake Publishers

Midas Touch

A number of objects are inside the mystery box. Put your hand inside the box and feel them. Don't peek! List the objects you can identify in the blanks below.

1. _____

2. _____

3. _____

4. _____

5. _____

6. _____

7. _____

8. _____

9. _____

10. _____

Which objects can be found in

nature? _____

_____

_____

Which objects are

manufactured? _____

_____

_____

Name _____

Forest Ranger

Find a leaf you like. Look at it closely. Answer the questions below about your leaf.

1. Where did you find your leaf? _____

2. Why did you choose this leaf? _____

3. What colors do you see in your leaf? _____

4. How does the leaf feel? _____

5. Is one side of the leaf rougher than the other side? _____

   If so, why do you think this is so? _____

   _____

6. What kind of tree does your leaf come from? (Use books your

   teacher provides to match your leaf to its tree.) _____

   _____

Make a leaf rubbing. Place a piece of paper over your leaf. With a crayon, gently rub until the outline of the leaf appears on the paper.

Quick 'N' Easy Learning Tasks, copyright © 1986 David S. Lake Publishers

is an
observant
scientist!

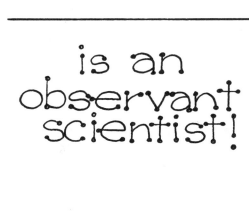

Quick 'N' Easy Learning Tasks, copyright © 1986 David S. Lake Publishers

SCIENCE
IS THE REAL THING

Health Tasks

Promote student awareness of good health habits with the poster, "Help Your Health!" Give the award to students who deserve recognition for practicing good health habits.

Special Reminders and Extra Materials

Task 1 How Do You Feel?: Provide a wall-mounted mirror for students to use. Each student will also need scissors and crayons or colored markers for the award certificate.

Task 2 Check Your Pulse: Students can share a stopwatch or use the classroom clock if it has a second hand.

Task 3 Take Your Temperature: Students can share a thermometer strip, which is available at most drugstores.

Task 4 Measure Yourself: Attach a growth chart or tape measure to a classroom wall for students to use. Provide a colored pencil.

Task 5 Vision Check: Mount a Snellen eye chart, which most school nurses can provide, on a wall. Mark a spot on the floor exactly 20 feet away from the chart. Students will stand at this spot to check their vision. Provide a 4" × 4" construction-paper eye patch for students to use in covering an eye during their vision check.

Task 6 Sleep Keeper: Make a class sleep chart like the sample below. Post this on a wall or bulletin board so students can enter information daily for a week.

Task 7 Brush Your Teeth!: Each student should have a toothbrush with his or her name on it and a tooth discoloring tablet (available from most dentists or local dental-health associations). Students can share a tube of toothpaste. Have students brush their teeth at the classroom or restroom sink. Provide a mirror.

NUMBER OF HOURS SLEPT LAST NIGHT

Student Name	Monday	Tuesday	Wednesday	Thursday	Friday
Pat					
Colleen					

Name _____

How Do You Feel?

1. Look in the mirror.
   Is your face rosy or pale? _____

2. Feel your forehead.
   Is it warm, hot, or cold? _____

3. Touch your eyelids.
   Do your eyes hurt or burn? _____

4. Feel your stomach.
   Does it hurt? _____

5. Do you feel healthy and happy? _____
   If so, color and cut out the good health
   certificate below.

I Feel Fit
as a
Fiddle
Today !

name _____

date _____

Quick 'N' Easy Learning Tasks, copyright © 1986 David S. Lake Publishers

Check Your Pulse

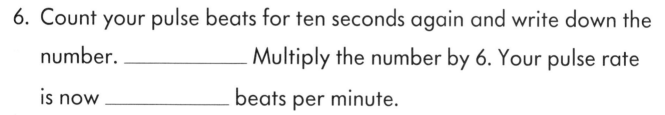

1. Press two fingers on the inside of your wrist to find your pulse.

2. Count your pulse beats for ten seconds. (Use a clock or watch.)

3. Write down the number of beats

   you counted. _____

4. Multiply the above number by 6, and write down your answer.

   _____ This is your pulse

   rate. It is _____ beats

   per minute.

5. Jog in place 25 times. Then sit down.

6. Count your pulse beats for ten seconds again and write down the

   number. _____ Multiply the number by 6. Your pulse rate

   is now _____ beats per minute.

7. Is your pulse rate faster or slower after jogging?

   _____

8. Why do you think there is a difference between your resting

   and jogging pulse rates? _____

   _____

   _____

Name _____

Take Your Temperature

1. Place the thermometer strip on your forehead for two minutes. (Watch the clock!)

2. After two minutes, remove the strip and read your temperature. Write your temperature here. _____ Your normal temperature is 98.6°.

3. Draw a picture of how you think you would look if your temperature were 102°.

Quick 'N' Easy Learning Tasks, copyright © 1986 David S. Lake Publishers

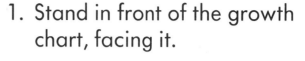

Measure Yourself

1. Stand in front of the growth chart, facing it.

2. Hold the length of a colored pencil straight across the top of your head and mark your height on the chart.

3. How many inches tall are

   you? _____

4. Now figure your height in feet and inches. (Reminder: 12 inches = 1 foot)

   I am _____ feet and

   _____ inches tall.

5. Tell your height to a friend. Find out your friend's height. Is your friend taller or shorter than you, or are you and your friend the same

   height? _____

Vision Check

1. Stand twenty feet away from the eye chart. (See mark on floor.)

2. Read the top row (row 1) of the eye chart with both eyes. Write the letter you see.

   _____

3. Read another row. Write in

   order the letters you see. _____

4. Which row has the smallest letters? _____
   Can you read the letters in this row at

   twenty feet? _____

   If so, write in order the letters you see.

   _____

5. Find the "20-20" row. Read it with both eyes. Write in order

   the letters you see. _____

6. Now cover your left eye with an eye patch and read the
   "20-20" row with your right eye. Write in order the letters

   you see. _____

7. Now cover your right eye and read the "20-20" row with
   your left eye. Write in order the letters you see.

   _____

8. Does one eye have better sight than the other? _____

Quick 'N' Easy Learning Tasks, copyright © 1986 David S. Lake Publishers

Name _____

Sleep Keeper

1. Are you tired? _____

2. What time did you go to sleep last night? _____

3. What time did you wake up this morning? _____

4. How many hours did you sleep last night? _____

   Do you think that was enough sleep? _____

   Why or why not? _____

   _____

5. Record on the sleep chart below the number of hours you slept last night. Keep a record of your sleep habits for one week.

Number of hours slept last night	Monday	Tuesday	Wednesday	Thursday	Friday

6. Which night did you get the most sleep? _____

   the least sleep? _____

   Did getting more sleep make you a better student the next day?

   _____

Brush Your Teeth!

Brush your teeth at the sink. Then answer these questions.

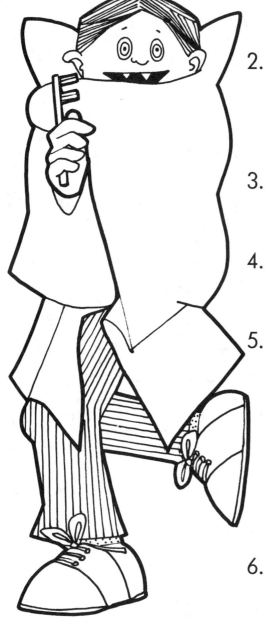

1. In what direction did you brush your upper teeth? _____

   Why? _____

2. In what direction did you brush your lower teeth? _____

   Why? _____

3. How many times did you rinse your mouth after brushing? _____

4. Does your mouth feel better now that you've brushed your teeth? _____

5. Get a tooth discoloring tablet from your teacher. Put it in your mouth and chew it. Now look in the mirror at your teeth. The coloring from the tablet will discolor your teeth where you have not brushed thoroughly. Brush your teeth again, paying special attention to the discolored areas.

6. What else can you do to clean your teeth better? _____

   _____

Quick 'N' Easy Learning Tasks, copyright © 1986 David S. Lake Publishers

Menu-Maker

Pick one item from each of the four food groups below to plan well-balanced meals for breakfast, lunch, and dinner.

VEGETABLES/FRUITS
apples
grapefruits
bananas
peaches
peas
broccoli
lettuce
carrots

MEATS/FISH/POULTRY	MILK/DAIRY	BREADS/CEREALS
eggs	cheese	crackers
lamb	milk	rolls
chicken	milk shake	wheat bread
beef	yogurt	corn flakes
veal	ice cream	cake
turkey	buttermilk	tortilla
salmon	butter	macaroni
halibut	sour cream	oatmeal

Breakfast Menu	Lunch Menu	Dinner Menu
_____	_____	_____
_____	_____	_____
_____	_____	_____
_____	_____	_____

Name _____

Let's Make Sense

Write the sense word on the line next to the correct body part. Use words from the word box.

Which sense do you think is most important? _____

Write some reasons you think this. _____

_____

_____

_____

Using Your Body

1. Eyes let us see beautiful things. List some of the beautiful things you see around you.

   _____

2. Ears let us hear. Listen for a minute and write down all the sounds you hear.

   _____

3. Your nose is for smelling. List some smells you are aware of throughout the day—from morning until night.

   _____

4. Teeth let us chew our food. List some foods that you need to chew before swallowing.

   _____

5. Your tongue is for tasting. Write down your favorite-tasting foods.

   _____

6. Hands are for touching. Look around you and notice the many different textures. Touch some things and describe how they feel —rough, smooth, or soft, for example.

   _____

7. Feet are for walking. List some other things you can do with your feet.

   _____

_____

practices
good health
habits!

_____

practices
good health
habits!

Quick 'N' Easy Learning Tasks, copyright © 1986 David S. Lake Publishers

Handwriting Tasks

Motivate your students to be aware of good handwriting with the poster, "Handwriting Is Write On!" Give the award to students who deserve recognition for their efforts and neatness.

Special Reminders and Extra Materials

Task 1 Print Out! and **Task 2** Cursive Capers!: Each student will need a pencil and a piece of lined paper.

Task 5 Name Tags: Reproduce the worksheet on heavy paper for durability. Each student will need scissors and crayons or colored markers.

Task 7 Bumper Sticker: Provide students with scissors, tape, and crayons or colored markers.

Task 8 Make-a-Sign: Reproduce the worksheet on heavy paper for durability. Each student will need scissors, tape, crayons or colored markers, and a flat wood stick for a sign handle.

Task 9 Good Deed Coupons: Provide scissors for each student.

Task 10 Coded Message: The coded message reads, "Because at night they become roosters."

Name _____

Print Out!

Practice printing the letters of the alphabet. First trace over the dotted lines of the letters with your pencil. Then print your own letters on another piece of paper.

Aa Bb Cc Dd Ee

Ff Gg Hh Ii Jj

Kk Ll Mm Nn Oo

Pp Qq Rr Ss Tt

Uu Vv

Ww Xx

Yy Zz

Quick 'N' Easy Learning Tasks, copyright © 1986 David S. Lake Publishers

Name _____

Cursive Capers!

Practice cursive writing. First trace over the dotted lines of the letters with your pencil. Then write your own letters on another piece of paper.

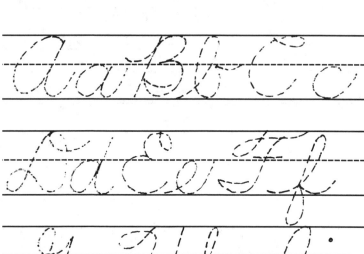

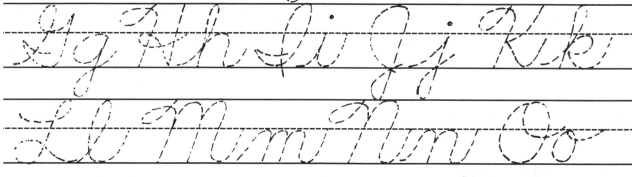

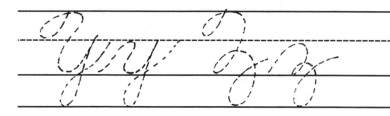

Name _____

Happy Days

Write the days of the week on the lines below. Use your best writing.

Monday --------------------------------

Tuesday --------------------------------

Wednesday --------------------------------

Thursday --------------------------------

Friday --------------------------------

Saturday --------------------------------

Sunday --------------------------------

Name _____

Year-at-a-Glance

Write the months of the year on the lines below.
Use your best writing.

January --------------------------------------

February -------------------------------------

March --

April --

May --

June ---

July ---

August ---------------------------------------

September ------------------------------------

October --------------------------------------

November -------------------------------------

December -------------------------------------

Name Tags

Make a name tag for yourself. Use a pencil to write your name on a tag below. Then trace over your letters with a crayon or colored marker. Cut out the tag and tape it on yourself. Make a name tag for a friend, too!

Name _____

Riddle Rage

Copy the riddles below. Use your best writing. Then write the answers to the riddles in the answer blanks. Look at the answers at the bottom of the page if you need help.

1. What monster will you find in your garden?

   _____

   _____

   Answer: _____

2. What cup is good to eat?

   _____

   _____

   Answer: _____

3. What animal will you always find in the library?

   _____

   _____

   Answer: _____

Answers: 1. a snapdragon   2. a cupcake   3. a bookworm

Quick 'N' Easy Learning Tasks, copyright © 1986 David S. Lake Publishers

Bumper Sticker

With a pencil, design a bumper sticker in the space below. Use your best writing. Then trace over your letters with crayons or colored markers. Cut out your bumper sticker along the dotted lines. Then tape it to a car (with the owner's permission, of course).

Name _____

Make-a-Sign

Make a sign to advertise something you like. It might be your favorite television show, game, or toy. Print your letters with a pencil. Trace over them and add other details with crayons or colored markers. Then cut out the sign and tape it to a stick holder.

Name _____

Good Deed Coupons

Do something special for someone you like. Write good deeds you wish to perform on the coupons below. Cut out the coupons along the dotted lines. Give them to your teacher, parents, grandparents, brothers, sisters, or friends.

I, _____ , will
(your name)

_____

_____

Date _____

_____
Signature

I, _____ , will
(your name)

_____

_____

Date _____

_____
Signature

I, _____ , will
(your name)

_____

_____

Date _____

_____
Signature

I, _____ , will
(your name)

_____

_____

Date _____

_____
Signature

Coded Message

To solve the riddle, use the code in the box. Write letters on the numbered lines below. Use your best handwriting.

ANSWER CODE

A = 26	J = 17	S = 8
B = 25	K = 16	T = 7
C = 24	L = 15	U = 6
D = 23	M = 14	V = 5
E = 22	N = 13	W = 4
F = 21	O = 12	X = 3
G = 20	P = 11	Y = 2
H = 19	Q = 10	Z = 1
I = 18	R = 9	

Riddle: Why do hens always lay eggs in the daytime?

___ ___ ___ ___ ___ ___ ___ ___ ___
25 22 24 26 6   8   22   26 7

___ ___ ___ ___ ___ ___ ___ ___ ___
13 18 20 19 7   7   19 22 2

___ ___ ___ ___ ___ ___
25 22 24 12 14 22

___ ___ ___ ___ ___ ___ ___ ___
9   12 12 8   7   22 9   8

uses good handwriting!

uses good handwriting!

Art Tasks

Stimulate your students to enjoy art activities with the poster. "I Love Art!" Give the award to students who deserve special recognition for particular art tasks.

Special Reminders and Extra Materials

Task 1 Ruler Art: Each student should have a ruler and pencil.

Task 5 Crayon Melt: An electric hot tray is required. You should supervise this activity closely. Tape a paper towel to the surface of the hot tray to keep it clean. Help students place their papers on the tray and draw crayon pictures. As they draw, the crayons will melt onto their papers.

Task 6 Jigsaw Puzzle: Reproduce this activity on heavy paper for durability. Each student should have scissors and crayons.

Task 8 Texture Rubbings: You and your students gather together objects suitable for making texture rubbings. Some possible items are string, paper clip, comb, piece of tree bark, coin, leaf, cloth, a zipper. Provide each student with crayons.

Task 9 Fingerprint Fun: Each student should have a set of watercolor paints and crayons or colored markers.

Task 10 Shape-a-Picture: Provide each student with scissors, paste, and crayons or colored markers.

Ruler Art

Use your ruler and pencil to draw a picture with only straight lines. Make some lines dark and others light, some long and others short. Use the space below

Draw-a-Picture

Draw a picture of your best friend.	Draw a picture of a dream you've had.
Draw a picture of your home.	Draw a picture of something you want.

Self-Portrait

Draw a picture of yourself doing something you like. Use this space.

Quick 'N' Easy Learning Tasks, copyright © 1986 David S. Lake Publishers

Name _____

Doodle Design

Make a doodle (scribble) on this
paper. What do you see? Try to think
of something it reminds you of. Turn
the doodle into a drawing.

Name _____

Crayon Melt

With your teacher's help, put this paper on the
hot tray. Draw a picture or design on the "hot"
paper with crayons. Watch the crayons melt as
you draw.

Jigsaw Puzzle

Draw and color a picture in the space below. Then cut it into pieces. Try to put your picture together again.

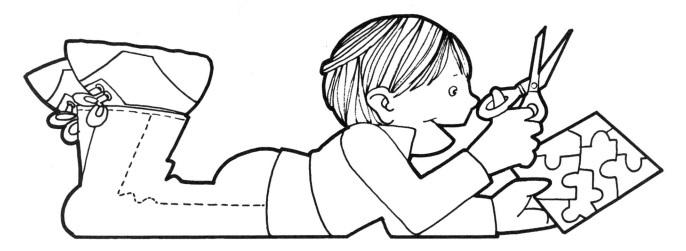

Quick 'N' Easy Learning Tasks, copyright © 1986 David S. Lake Publishers

Alphabet Art

Print some capital letters below.
Then change the letters into pictures.
Perhaps you can make flowers,
animals, buildings, or people.

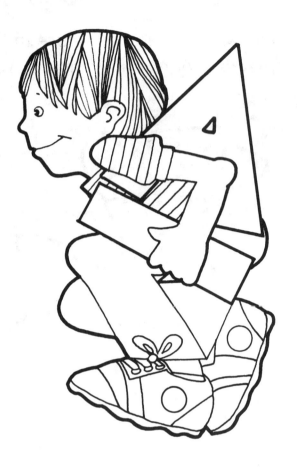

Quick 'N' Easy Learning Tasks, copyright © 1986 David S. Lake Publishers

Texture Rubbings

Choose an object and hold this paper on it. Gently rub your paper with the side of a crayon. You will see the object's form appear on the paper. Choose more objects and repeat the process several times. Use a different color crayon for each rubbing.

Name _____

Fingerprint Fun

Press a finger on damp watercolor paint. Then press your finger on this paper to make a fingerprint. Repeat this, using different fingers and colors. Make your prints into little creatures by adding details with crayons or colored markers.

Quick 'N' Easy Learning Tasks, copyright © 1986 David S. Lake Publishers

Name _____

Shape-a-Picture

Color and then cut out the shapes below. Arrange them on a piece of paper to form a picture. Paste them in place. Use crayons or colored markers to add details to your picture.

_____

is a super
artist!

_____

is a super
artist!

Send-Home Messages

SCIENCE

To _____

From _____

_____

_____

_____

HEALTH

To _____

From _____

_____

_____

_____

SOCIAL STUDIES

To _____

From _____

_____

_____

_____

Send-Home-Messages

ART

To _____

From _____

_____

_____

_____

SPELLING

d-e-a-r

To _____

From _____

_____

_____

_____

LANGUAGE ARTS

To _____

From _____

_____

_____

_____

Send-Home Messages

MATH

To _____

From _____

_____

_____

_____

READING

To _____

From _____

_____

_____

_____

HANDWRITING

To _____

From _____

_____

_____

_____